☀ The Christmas Eve Family Handbook ☀

D0792701

CIDER MILL PRESS

BOOK PUBLISHERS

Kennebunkport, Maine

Santa in A Box
Copyright © 2009 by Cider Mill Press Book Publishers, LLC

The Christmas Eve Family Handbook
Copyright © 2009 by Cider Mill Press Book Publishers, LLC

All rights reserved under the Pan-American and International Copyright Conventions.

No part of this book may be reproduced in whole or in part, scanned, photocopied, recorded, distributed in any printed or electronic form, or reproduced in any manner whatsoever, or by any information storage and retrieval system now known or hereafter invented, without express written permission of the publisher, except in the case of brief quotations embodied in critical articles and reviews.

The scanning, uploading, and distribution of this book via the Internet or via any other means without permission of the publisher is illegal and punishable by law. Please support authors' rights, and do not participate in or encourage piracy of copyrighted materials.

13-Digit ISBN: 978-1-60433-099-1
10-Digit ISBN: 1-60433-099-6

This book may be ordered by mail from the publisher. Please include $3.50 for postage and handling. Please support your local bookseller first!

Books published by Cider Mill Press Book Publishers are available at special discounts for bulk purchases in the United States by corporations, institutions, and other organizations. For more information, please contact the publisher.

Cider Mill Press Book Publishers
"Where good books are ready for press"
12 Port Farm Road
Kennebunkport, Maine 04046

Visit us on the Web!
www.cidermillpress.com

Design by Megan Rotondo
Typography: Adobe Garamond, Freehand 521 BT, Old Claude and OldEnglishEF
All illustrations courtesy of Jeff Albrecht
Printed in China

2 3 4 5 6 7 8 9 0

Table of Contents

❄ Chapter 1 ❄
Christmas Eve and the Magic of Santa

Santa in a Box is designed to get you and your family into the spirit of the season through the magic of Old Saint Nick. Gather your children, grandchildren, nieces, nephews, adult family members, friends, or neighbors around, put on the hat and beard, settle into a comfortable chair, and celebrate what the season represents when Santa is alive in it: wonder, merriment, the gift of real giving, and a most sincere "Ho, ho, ho!" There are so many ways to share the spirit of Santa, and this kit celebrates some of the very best—through stories, movies, treats, traditions, and memories.

You can choose to be Santa for one very special evening, or you can build the excitement leading up to Christmas Eve by choosing one activity a night for several consecutive nights. You may become so comfortable in your role as Santa that you find yourself in the true holiday spirit more than ever—perhaps visiting homebound elderly people, volunteering to wrap gifts for charity, performing a reading of "The Night Before Christmas" for a group of children, and even re-examining what Christmas means to you.

With this kit, let the spirit of Santa move you to delight others as you have so often been delighted by Santa yourself. You can put on the hat, beard and spectacles any time, but if you don't read the stories, watch the movies, savor making and eating the special treats, and embrace the traditions, you might as well ditch the Santa accessories and sport a "Bah, humbug!" button instead. A better idea, though, is to wear—and share—the contents of this box. There is no better way to get into the Christmas spirit.

✳ Chapter 2 ✳
The Magic of
Santa in Stories

The poem commonly known as "The Night Before Christmas" was first published in 1832 in the Troy (New York) *Sentinel* under its actual, original title, "A Visit from St. Nicholas." Since then it has become such a part of the Christmas season that almost everyone can recite at least a line or two.

When the poem was first published, people did not share a common idea of what Saint Nicholas looked like or what he did. Those perceptions depended on your family's national origin—whether German, French, Dutch, English, and so on. Each tradition was a bit different. But when Clement C. Moore described the man who came down the chimney, the image of Santa Claus as we now know him—"dressed all in fur," with twinkling eyes, "cheeks like roses," a "nose like a cherry," and a beard "white as snow"—was fixed forever.

It wasn't until many years after its publication that Moore was credited as author of the poem. It is reproduced here in full so that you can continue a nearly 200-year-old tradition and share it with your family.

The Night Before Christmas (A Visit From St. Nicholas)

By Clement C. Moore

'Twas the night before Christmas,
    when all through the house
Not a creature was stirring, not even a mouse;
The stockings were hung by the chimney with care,
In hopes that St. Nicholas soon would be there;

The children were nestled all snug in their beds,
While visions of sugar-plums danced in their heads;

And Mama in her kerchief, and I in my cap,
Had just settled down for a long winter's nap—

When out on the lawn there arose such a clatter,
I sprang from the bed to see what was the matter:
Away to the window I flew like a flash,
Tore open the shutters and threw up the sash.

The moon on the breast of the new-fallen snow
Gave the luster of mid-day to objects below
When, what to my wondering eyes should appear,
But a miniature sleigh, and eight tiny reindeer,

With a little old driver, so lively and quick,
I knew in a moment it must be St. Nick.
More rapid than eagles his coursers they came,
And he whistled, and shouted,
    and called them by name;

"Now, Dasher! Now, Dancer!
Now, Prancer and Vixen!
On, Comet! On, Cupid! On, Donder and Blitzen!
To the top of the porch! To the top of the wall!
Now dash away! Dash away! Dash away, all!"

As dry leaves that before the wild hurricane fly
When they meet with an obstacle, mount to the sky,
So up to the house-top the coursers they flew,
With the sleigh full of toys, and St. Nicholas, too.

And then, in a twinkling, I heard on the roof
The prancing and pawing of each little hoof.
As I drew in my head, and was turning around,
Down the chimney St. Nicholas came with a bound.

He was dressed all in fur, from his head to his foot,
And his clothes were all tarnished with ashes and soot;
A bundle of toys he had flung on his back,

And he looked like a peddler just opening his pack.
His eyes—how they twinkled! His dimples—how merry!
His cheeks were like roses, his nose like a cherry;
His droll little mouth was drawn up like a bow,
And the beard of his chin was as white as the snow.

The stump of a pipe he held tight in his teeth,
And the smoke it encircled his head like a wreath.
He had a broad face and a little round belly
That shook, when he laughed, like a bowlful of jelly.

He was chubby and plump, a right jolly old elf,
And I laughed when I saw him, in spite of myself;
A wink of his eye and a twist of his head
Soon gave me to know I had nothing to dread;

He spoke not a word, but went straight to his work
And filled all the stockings, then turned with a jerk,
And laying his finger aside of his nose
And giving a nod, up the chimney he rose;

He sprang to his sleigh, to his team gave a whistle,
And away they all flew like the down of a thistle.

But I heard him exclaim, ere he drove out of sight,

"Happy Christmas to all, and to all a good-night."

Chapter 3 ❄
The Magic of
Santa in Movies

Just as it has become a special tradition for many families to enjoy together the reading of "The Night Before Christmas," so, too, for many has it become a tradition to gather in front of the television to share a favorite Christmas movie.

There is something very comforting about snuggling under a warm blanket together to watch a great Christmas movie as a family. With mugs of hot chocolate and bowls of popcorn at the ready, it's time to push "play" on the remote and settle in. The only difficult part will be deciding which one to watch first!

Rudolph the Red-Nosed Reindeer
Can't you just hear the sleigh bells jingling in the background as the singing snowman (Burl Ives) introduces this wonderful story? The version that many are most familiar with is the 1964 television special, but the story was created back in 1939 and first sung as a song in 1949. No matter; the Rudolph we know and love is the one that captures Clarisse's heart when she says, "I think you're cute." Rudolph and Clarisse are part of a great cast of characters that includes Yukon Cornelius, Herbie the Dentist, and, of course, the Abominable Snowman. With songs and sentiments for the whole family, this is at the top of the list.

Santa Claus Is Coming to Town

Another vintage television special that has become a perennial favorite is this 1970 stop-motion production using characters crafted from wooden models. With Fred Astaire as the voice of S.D. Kluger, the narrator, and Mickey Rooney as the young Kris Kringle, it sets to music the story that was first broadcast on radio in 1934. What a film!

A Christmas Carol

This story of Ebenezer Scrooge and his transformation from disdaining to embracing the spirit of Christmas is so well known that it wouldn't feel like Christmas without watching it at some point in December. The story is based on the book by Charles Dickens first published in 1843 as *A Christmas Carol in Prose, Being a Ghost Story of Christmas.* It is a favorite of community theater companies and a treat to see performed live. But there are lots of great film versions as well. You can't go wrong with the ones starring Patrick Stewart or George C. Scott, and there's the classic British version with Alistair Sim—a real heartwarmer in black and white.

A Charlie Brown Christmas

The *Peanuts* comics strip gang created by Charles Schultz comes alive in this Christmas tale about seeing beyond the commercialization of Christmas. It originally aired on CBS in 1965 and earned both an Emmy and a Peabody award. For over 40 years families have laughed and cried as Charlie Brown's vision of the true meaning of Christmas is finally realized through his mishaps and the perspectives of Lucy, Linus, Schroeder, Pigpen, and everyone's favorite, Snoopy.

How the Grinch Stole Christmas

No other Dr. Seuss book has so captured our hearts and

imaginations as this one, published in 1957. A wonderful story in and of itself—also worthy of reading aloud in your *Santa in a Box* costume—the 1966 animated version with Boris Karloff playing the voice of the Grinch is the ultimate telling of the tale. The Grinch's dog Max even gives Snoopy a run for his money as the cutest Christmas canine. A film version starring Jim Carrey was released in 2000.

It's a Wonderful Life

This 1946 movie is a little long, and it rambles, but it is a heartwarming tearjerker that for some is a must-see at Christmastime. It is the story of a man (George Bailey, played by James Stewart) who considers suicide but through flashbacks of his life provided by a guardian angel is able to see all the lives he's touched. It was named one of "100 Best American Films" by the American Film Institute. And where else can you learn how an angel earns their wings?

Frosty the Snowman

This animated classic has been entertaining families since it first aired on CBS in 1969. Produced by Rankin/Bass, the same folks who created the TV version of *Rudolph the Red-Nosed Reindeer*, it was another huge hit, and it is still a huge hit with the littlest members of the family, who love all the magic this wonderful tale offers up.

Miracle on 34th Street

The ultimate Santa movie, this film's central theme is the question of whether a certain Macy's department store Santa might be the real thing. For real heartwarming, down-to-earth cynicism and the ultimate happy ending, you can't beat the original black-and-white 1947 version with Natalie Wood and Maureen O'Hara. A colorized version was released in 1994.

The Polar Express
The book came out in 1985 and became an instant hit, winning a Caldecott Medal for children's literature. It's the story of a boy who rides a magic train to the North Pole and brings home the spirit of Christmas. The 2004 film version starring Tom Hanks as the train's conductor is as beautiful and inspiring as the book.

Home Alone
This 1990 release was a mega-hit that launched the career of its star, Macaulay Culkin. When his family heads off to a Christmas vacation in France but accidentally leaves him behind, young Kevin realizes every kid's dream: to have the house to himself. But the dream turns sad, and even scary, as two erstwhile thugs try to rob his home. It's a great tale of hi-jinks and hilarity enjoyed by children of all ages.

❄ Chapter 4 ❄
Santa-Inspired Goodies

Many delicious foods traditionally grace family tables at Christmastime, often reflecting cultural or national heritage. Other dishes and treats become holiday traditions simply because they're family favorites.

❄ The Best Cup of Hot ❄ Cocoa in the World

No matter a family's background or the ages of family members, a cup of hot chocolate is a universal favorite.

Be prepared to learn the secret for a best-ever cup of cocoa!

Hot chocolate (also known as hot cocoa, drinking chocolate, or just cocoa) is a heated beverage that typically consists of shaved chocolate or cocoa powder, heated water or milk (versions include half-and-half, skimmed milk, whole milk, or chocolate milk), and sugar. While hot chocolate is generally a drink consumed for pleasure, recent studies have suggested that it also provides health benefits because of antioxidants that can be found in cocoa. (Until the 19th century, in fact, hot chocolate was used medicinally to treat ailments such as stomach diseases.)

It is believed that chocolate was first enjoyed as a beverage by the Mayan peoples of South America around 2,000 years ago. A cocoa beverage was an essential part of Aztec culture by A.D 1400. The drink became popular in Europe after being introduced from Mexico, and it has undergone multiple changes since then. Today, hot chocolate is consumed throughout the world and is prepared differently in different countries, as well as in different households!

Below is the basic recipe, with variations following.

BASIC HOT COCOA

Ingredients:
1/2 cup sugar
1/4 cup unsweetened cocoa powder
Dash salt
1/3 cup hot water
4 cups (1 qt.) milk
3/4 teaspoon vanilla extract

Miniature marshmallows or sweetened whipped cream (optional)

Directions:
1. Stir together sugar, cocoa, and salt in medium saucepan, then stir in water to dissolve dry ingredients and make a liquid base. Cook over medium heat, stirring constantly, until mixture comes to a boil. Reduce heat and add milk, stirring constantly. Do not allow it to boil after adding the milk!
2. Remove from heat and add vanilla extract. Beat with rotary beater or whisk until foamy. Serve topped with marshmallows or whipped cream, if desired. Makes five 8-ounce servings.

CREAMIER HOT COCOA
Use half-and-half or whipping cream instead of regular milk.

MAPLE SYRUP COCOA
Swap ¾ cup of maple syrup for the sugar. (For even more of a taste treat, use Grade B dark maple syrup.)

PEPPERMINT COCOA
Add 1 well-crushed, whole candy cane at the time you add the vanilla extract.

CINNAMON COCOA
Two versions:
Serve with a whole cinnamon stick in the cup or mug to be used as a stirrer.
OR:
Add 1/8 teaspoon ground cinnamon and 1/8 teaspoon ground nutmeg when you add the vanilla.

MOCHA COCOA

Two versions:

Add one shot of espresso!

OR:

If you don't have espresso, add 2 to 2 1/2 teaspoons powdered instant coffee when you add the vanilla extract.

❄ Reindeer Treats ❄ (Kids love these, too!)

Truth be told, there are exactly two kinds of mixes reindeer love to eat: the salty kind and the semi-salty kind. Make either, and Rudolph, Dasher, Dancer, Prancer, Vixen, Comet, Cupid, Donder, and especially Blitzen will all come running once they get a sniff!

Add to the magic by putting the mix in individual bags with the reindeers' names on them.

SALTY-BUTTERY REINDEER MIX

Ingredients:

2 cups Bugles® snacks
1 cup Cheez-It® crackers
1 cup pretzel sticks
2 cups Corn Chex® cereal
1 cup bite-size Shredded
    Wheat® cereal
1 cup salted peanuts
1 cup pecan halves
1/2 cup butter, melted
1 tablespoon maple syrup
1/4 teaspoon black pepper
1/4 teaspoon salt

Directions:
In a large bowl, combine the first seven ingredients. In another bowl, combine the butter, syrup, salt, and pepper. Heat in microwave 15–20 seconds. Pour over cereal mixture and toss to coat.

Transfer to ungreased 15 x 10 x 1-inch baking pan. Bake uncovered at 250° for 1 hour, stirring every 15 minutes.

Yield: about 9 cups

SALTY-SWEET POPCORN REINDEER BLEND

Ingredients:
2 cups M&M's® candies
1 cups pretzel sticks
2 cups Corn Chex® cereal
4 cups hot buttered popcorn
1 cup raisins
1 cup salted peanuts
1/4 teaspoon salt

Directions:
In a large bowl, combine first six ingredients. Sprinkle with salt and mix thoroughly.

Yield: about 11 cups

❄ Cookies for Santa ❄

It's no secret that Santa appreciates treats, and these cookies are sure to sweeten anyone's holiday mood!

CANDY CANE COOKIES

These taste as yummy as they look and are fun to make. Keep an eye on them while they bake to make sure they don't overcook on the bottom.

Ingredients:
1/2 cup butter (1 stick, or ¼ pound), softened
1/2 cup shortening
1 cup confectioner's sugar
1 egg
1 1/2 tsp. almond extract
1 tsp. vanilla
2 1/2 cups flour
1 tsp. salt
1/2 tsp. red food coloring

Directions:
Heat oven to 375°. Thoroughly combine butter, shortening, confectioner's sugar, egg, and almond and vanilla extracts. Mix salt into the flour in a measuring cup, then add to butter mixture gradually until it combines to make a soft dough.
Divide dough in half, and blend red food coloring into one half.
Shape 1 teaspoon of dough from each half into 4-inch rope. (For smooth, even ropes, roll them back and forth on a lightly floured board.) Place the two ropes side by side, press together lightly, and twist to make each cookie. Place cookies on ungreased baking sheet, curving the top

of each cookie down to form the handle of the cane. Bake about 9 minutes or until set and "white" stripes are very light brown in color.

If you wish, mix 1/2 cup crushed peppermint candy with 1/2 cup granulated sugar, and when cookies are out of the oven, immediately sprinkle with candy mixture and remove from baking sheet.

Makes about 4 dozen cookies.

The Christmas Pickle

Long ago it was customary to use a real pickle for this holiday tradition, but it's much easier (and less smelly, for sure!) to use a glass ornament shaped like a pickle.

Here's how it goes: On Christmas Eve, designate one person to hide the green pickle ornament somewhere on the Christmas tree so that it will be hard to find. The pickle's location is to be kept secret. Then, on Christmas morning, after all the presents under the tree have been opened, ask the kids (and anyone else who's visiting) to find the pickle on the tree. The first person to find it gets a special gift such as an extra present, money, or a special privilege like staying up late or dinner at a favorite restaurant—whatever the household deems appropriate and fun!

❄ *Chapter 5* ❄
Keeping Santa Alive in Your Heart and Home

Holiday readings, movies, treats—all are wonderful ways to reinforce the traditions of Christmas and Christmas Eve. But you don't have to stop there. Following are some ideas for other fun and rewarding ways to make your family's holiday experience even richer. You can pick and choose and add to this list to personalize it. You might even start a few new family holiday traditions.

❄ 10 More Family Holiday ❄ Activities You Can Try

1. Go Christmas caroling
2. Make and send handmade Christmas cards
3. Play a board game
4. Volunteer time to a local charity organization
5. Sponsor a cookie swap
6. Organize a grab-bag event
7. Make a gingerbread house
8. Walk around your neighborhood and look at Christmas lights and decorations
9. Go to a religious service
10. Make colorful garlands from popcorn and cranberries or colored construction paper

❄ About Cider Mill Press ❄
Book Publishers

Good ideas ripen with time. From seed to harvest, Cider Mill Press strives to bring fine reading, information, and entertainment together between the covers of its creatively crafted books. Our Cider Mill bears fruit twice a year, publishing a new crop of titles each spring and fall.

CIDER MILL
PRESS

BOOK
PUBLISHERS

Visit us on the Web at
www.cidermillpress.com
or write to us at
12 Port Farm Road
Kennebunkport, Maine 04046